GARAGE BANDS™

HOW TO START YOUR OWN BAND

DANIEL E. HARMON

rosen publishing's
rosen
central®

NEW YORK

Published in 2012 by The Rosen Publishing Group, Inc.
29 East 21st Street, New York, NY 10010

Library of Congress Cataloging-in-Publication Data

Harmon, Daniel E.
How to start your own band/Daniel E. Harmon.—1st ed.
     p. cm.—(Garage bands)
Includes bibliographical references and index.
ISBN 978-1-4488-5657-2 (library binding)—
ISBN 978-1-4488-5661-9 (pbk.)—
ISBN 978-1-4488-5665-7 (6-pack)
1. Rock groups—Vocational guidance—Juvenile literature. I. Title.
ML3795.H32 2012
781.64023—dc22

                                                                    2011011906

Manufactured in the United States of America

CPSIA Compliance Information: Batch #W12YA: For further information, contact Rosen Publishing, New York, New York, at 1-800-237-9932.

CONTENTS

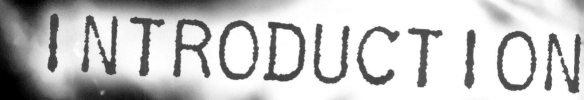

INTRODUCTION

Rock star Tom Petty began playing in bands as a teenager during the mid-1960s. The Beatles had just launched the "British invasion" of rock music around the world, and millions of young people like Petty wanted to emulate them.

"It was no real challenge to start a group then," Petty recalled in the book *Start Your Own Band*, written by his longtime friend Marty Jourard. "All you needed was four guys, some guitars and drums, and a garage."

If anything, it's even simpler to start a band today. For one thing, you don't have to be a guy; popular girl bands are everywhere. You don't necessarily need guitars and drums; teen bands adapt all sorts of instrumental

A BASIC GARAGE BAND USUALLY INCLUDES A VOCALIST, ELECTRIC GUITARIST, AND DRUMMER. IN TIME, MOST BANDS INCLUDE AN ELECTRIC BASS PLAYER AND ONE OR MORE ADDITIONAL INSTRUMENTS.

combinations and create styles of music not yet conceived when Petty was a teenager. Although a garage with available space is convenient, it isn't required; bands rehearse in living rooms, bedrooms, and kitchens, and in public school, church, and community facilities.

While it's easy to form a music group, it isn't at all easy to succeed. Band members must practice religiously, both individually and as a unit. They have to work at getting along when problems arise and progress is sluggish. The test is to stay together long enough to come up with a meaningful sound that audiences will appreciate.

Making music is an intimate form of creative expression. It's a way to convey a personal message—to share joys, express concerns, and tell stories. Music, especially loud music, can be a creative way to vent bad feelings—anger, fear, annoyance, and sorrow. In the meantime, it's a way to demonstrate your talents in public. In the process of developing a following of fans, band members contribute to the mushrooming body of popular music. They can realize an exhilarating sense of personal accomplishment.

Do you find yourself perpetually tapping your feet or dancing to music? Lip-synching lyrics in front of your bedroom mirror? Playing "air guitar" or "invisible drumsticks," unmindful of whether anyone is watching? Is music in your blood—and your brain, hands, and voice? If so, a band just might be where you belong.

There is no formula for a band's success, because all musicians are unique. In fact, many musicians take great pride in their distinctive personalities and habits. Different roads lead to stardom. There are certain common requirements, though, for musical excellence. Members of a band, like members of any team, must be willing to compromise, learn from one another, work together, and persevere.

Whatever your motive for making music, it should be fun as well as work. Although some musicians, young and old, prefer to play alone, music can be more fun in a band than in a solo performance. Many budding instrumentalists and singers discover that by creating music with friends, they can multiply the enjoyment. There is a special sense of achievement in building a sound together. Playing in a band is a wonderful way to cultivate friendships, be creative, have a lot of fun, and maybe even travel, earn money, and experience a bit of fame.

YOU AND YOUR MUSIC

CHAPTER ONE
GARAGE BAND PASS

Many professional musicians grew up in musical families. Their parents were touring and recording artists. Older siblings were talented singers or instrumentalists who performed solo or in bands. An uncle, aunt, or cousin may have been a gifted electric guitarist or keyboardist.

Others were influenced and taught by friends. They spent much of their time sitting in on rehearsals, absorbed in the sound, marveling at their friends' skills. They became groupies, attending every performance of their musician friends.

Some, though, had no one close to teach and inspire them. Their musical interests grew as they simply listened. In order to learn, they took music lessons. A few were largely self-taught.

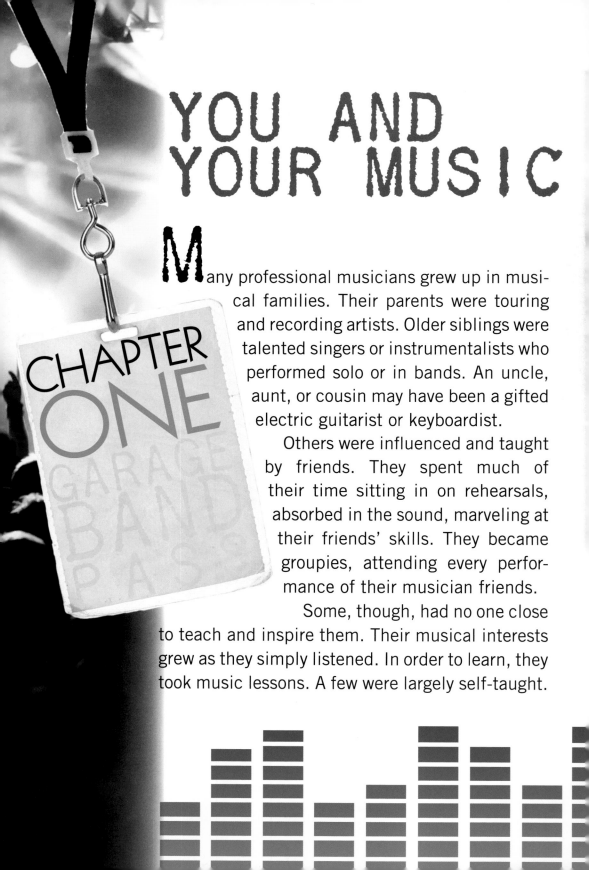

ELECTRIC GUITARISTS EXCHANGE IDEAS INSIDE A STUDIO. MOST BEGINNING INSTRUMENTALISTS LEARN FROM EXPERIENCED PLAYERS, FRIENDS, RELATIVES, OR PAID INSTRUCTORS. SOME LEARN WITH INSTRUCTIONAL VIDEOS.

Whether you are following in the footsteps of another musician or pursuing music on your own, you must understand what's involved in producing music worth hearing. If you want to start or join a band, you must have something to contribute.

You have a strong interest in music and at least a kernel of talent, or you wouldn't be reading this book. What does it take to become a valuable member—perhaps leader—of a band?

Successful Musicians Have a Few Things in Common

No two musicians are alike. They come from different musical backgrounds, begin at different ages, learn in different ways, and acquire different musical interests. But most serious musicians share several common traits.

A Love of Music (Naturally)

Music becomes a special passion—not merely an interest—in their lives. This is not to say they'll commit to a professional musical career. The determination to play music, though, is central to them.

Eventually, they focus on a particular type of music. At the same time, serious musicians cultivate a basic knowledge and appreciation of other musical styles. They learn from other musicians, including those with different tastes. They pay attention to sound effects, instrumental techniques, and the ways that instruments and voices blend. They learn to apply some of these ideas in developing their own sounds.

Talent

Most people have at least a slight degree of musical ability. Even if they can't sing on pitch, they can learn to play an instrument. Instrumentation is essentially a matter of keeping count, keeping a steady beat, and executing moves with fingers, hands, and arms. Learning an instrument is, by and large, a process of mechanical steps and sequences.

The key is to develop raw talent into performance skills. Some individuals must practice longer and harder than others. But with determination, they all can arrive competently onstage.

A DRUMMER PRACTICES ON AN ELECTRIC DRUM KIT. LEARNING AN INSTRUMENT IS BASICALLY A MATTER OF PHYSICAL COORDINATION COMBINED WITH STEADY TIMING. MASTERING IT REQUIRES SPECIAL TALENT AND PERSEVERANCE.

Willingness to Work Hard

Even the most gifted musicians have to work. Their playing and singing may seem effortless to observers, but constant effort is required in order for them to deliver their very best performances. Professional musicians in their seventies, eighties, and nineties continue to practice regularly.

Determination and Dedication

Musical accomplishment is a long-term endeavor. Don't expect to apply yourself only for as long as it takes to get a few gigs behind you, and then coast the rest of your life. All musicians experience discouragement and disappointment. Their response to setbacks is an indicator of their likelihood to succeed. Attitude is as important as ability.

Singer? Songwriter? Soloist?

Some musically inclined people are good singers. They love to participate in choruses and choirs, and they enjoy the thrill of singing occasional solos. They have little desire, though, to learn an instrument or join a band.

Others are writers. They pen poems and set some of their lyrics to music. (If you're serious about songwriting, you can find extensive help and ideas in books such as Stephen Citron's *Songwriting: A Complete Guide to the Craft*.)

Many young people are gifted and eager to express themselves through music, but they aren't cut out for band membership. Natural loners can be happy, successful musicians. Self-reliant, they're unwilling to compromise their tastes or work with other musicians. They learn to accompany themselves on guitar or piano.

Eddie McCloud, a songwriter, multi-instrumentalist, poet, and painter in Lexington, South Carolina, has played piano in a

WHAT IS A GARAGE BAND?

The definition of "garage band" has become complicated. *Merriam-Webster's Collegiate Dictionary* defines it as "an amateur rock band typically holding its rehearsals in a garage and usually having only a local audience." Someone first coined the term in the early 1970s.

The online dictionary WordIQ (http://www.wordiq.com) describes garage bands as "startup bands, often consisting of teenagers and twenty-somethings. The term is derived from the phenomenon of startup bands literally playing in the garages of houses." Another Internet dictionary, Reverso (http://dictionary.reverso.net), identifies a garage band as "a rough-and-ready amateurish rock group (perhaps from the practice of such bands rehearsing in a garage)."

Many startup ensembles don't have a garage available. They gather in someone's basement, living room, or attic, or maybe in a vacant corner of a warehouse owned by a parent or friend. Those groups might be considered garage bands, too.

Another problem with labeling a garage band is that some amateur musicians don't play rock music. They're interested in jazz, country, blues, acoustic pop, or another musical genre.

The definition of a garage band really is challenged if the group becomes widely known. Once an amateur group begins performing in public and earning money, is it still a garage band?

performing group. However, he prefers to create fantastic sounds in his home studio. He writes songs and records them methodically. He puts down a basic track, with keyboard or guitar accompanying his vocals. Then he adds bass, mandolin, melodica, harmony vocals, and other tracks. McCloud

SONGWRITING AND PERFORMING ARE SERIOUS ENDEAVORS THAT REQUIRE MUCH MORE WORK OFFSTAGE THAN ON. HERE, AN ACOUSTIC GUITARIST MAKES NOTES ABOUT CHORD POSITIONS.

loves his multiple roles: songwriter, singer, entire band, arranger, producer, and studio technician.

The Internet, especially YouTube, gives blossoming musicians like McCloud broad exposure. Locally, he finds open mike events invaluable. "You can see how the crowd reacts to your playing and how they react to your original material."

Some soloists are extraordinary virtuosos on guitars, keyboards, and other instruments. Some simply love to sing in the shower and hum while doing homework.

Many young musicians, though, aspire to perform with a group. Exciting sounds bang around in their heads—ideas for arranging two or more instruments, vocal harmonies, guitar riffs, drum rhythms, or horn or keyboard solos. They need to be in a band.

The Right Band for You

Young people generally think of rock 'n' roll when they think of a band. The basic instruments are electric guitar, electric bass, and drums. Electronic keyboards and acoustic rhythm guitars are common accessory instruments.

If you're talented with another instrument, you can still find a place. Pianos, violins, brass and reed instruments, bagpipes, harmonicas, mandolins, tambourines—practically every musical instrument has been used in rock music.

Moreover, rock isn't the only style of popular music. Some bands use all-acoustic instrumentation, including stringed (orchestral) rather than electric bass. Many aspiring musicians want to become country stars. Some find their passion jamming in jazz combos. A guitarist may prefer bluegrass-style flat-picking, folk-style finger-picking, or soulful blues solos rather than throbbing rock riffs.

No doubt you're interested in a particular instrument. Guitar players draw the most attention. Possibly, you envision yourself onstage, the lights dimming around you, launching into a phenomenal twelve-minute solo riff while your bandmates exit the stage and take a break. But after a few months struggling with your first guitar, you may decide it really isn't your instrument. Your fingers aren't long enough or strong enough, or you aren't good at changing chords, or you're unwilling to trim your fingernails.

Keep an open mind. Experiment with various instruments until you find the one that's just right for you.

You may have to work at a steady job or at odd jobs for months to save enough money for a good instrument. A usable beginner guitar costs $200 or less. Electronic keyboards and drum kits typically cost more than $1,000.

It's important to invest in a good-quality instrument. Even a beginner instrument must be easily playable. A guitar that's physically hard to play or refuses to stay in tune will discourage your interest in music. Ask an experienced musician to help you shop.

Prepare Yourself

After you decide on your instrument, your work begins in earnest. You need to become competent before you'll be of value to a band. The best musicians never stop practic-ing, even after they become successful.

Some instrumentalists learn the basics from a parent, older brother or sister, or experienced friend and begin to develop their own style. Others progress much faster by taking private or group lessons. Instruction books and audiovisual training aids are available for every instrument. Much of this material can be checked out of a library, rented from a music store, or borrowed from friends.

The very best lessons, though, are worthless without regular practice. That takes determination and discipline. Too many music students, young and old, seem to believe the $20 or $30 a week they pay for lessons should "buy" them all the skills they need. The only time they spend with their instruments is during the lesson; they never rehearse at home. They make slow (or no) progress, soon become bored, and abandon their musical pursuits.

Special Considerations

As you prepare yourself to join a band, there are two related matters to consider. One is musical, the other personal.

First, should you learn to read musical notation? Many performers never do, but it's a good skill to have. The ability to read and write music makes it easier to learn new material and arrange songs.

Second, obtain buy-in from the important people in your life. "Buy-in" is a business planning term. If office

MUSICIANS NEED MORAL SUPPORT. IF YOU DECIDE TO PURSUE MUSIC SERIOUSLY, KEEP YOUR FAMILY AND FRIENDS INFORMED OF YOUR PROGRESS, MAKING THEM PART OF YOUR SUPPORT TEAM.

managers want to install a new computer system or offer a new service, they need to persuade workers at every level to "buy into" the idea. Otherwise, the change will be difficult if not impossible.

If you want to be a band musician, you need to make certain people understand it's something you really need to do—and it won't create trouble for them. Those key individuals include your family, who will have to get used to your practice noise. They also include nonmusician friends, with whom you probably won't be spending as much time.

BUILDING A BAND

There is no instrumental or vocal formula for the makeup of a band. Different bands use different combinations of instruments and voices.

Typically, a band originates around two or three musicians who already have selected their instruments and learned the basics and who share interests in the same kind of music. They want to discover what they sound like together and begin jamming in a living room or bedroom.

When they become serious about starting a band, they look for additional musicians—and additional space. A full-fledged band eventually will need a larger room, such as a garage or basement.

Bands often begin as family affairs. Two or more brothers, sisters, or cousins—perhaps parents and

CHAPTER
TWO
GARAGE
BAND
PASS

A TENNESSEE BAND PERFORMS AT A SUMMER MUSIC FESTIVAL. NOTICE A COMMON TECHNIQUE FOR ESTABLISHING NAME RECOGNITION: THE LETTERS KOL ON THE BASS DRUM ARE THE INITIALS OF THE BAND, KINGS OF LEON.

children—spend time making music together. They gradually perfect their skills, build repertoires of songs, and invite other musicians to join them.

Before they begin building a band, the founders need to answer key questions. First, what style of music do they want to make—or are they open to a variety of styles?

Second, what instruments will they need—and will theirs be a vocal or all-instrumental band? If vocal, will there be one lead singer, or will different singers alternate? How important are harmony vocals to the sound they have in mind? (Singers who can harmonize are not as easy to find as those who can carry a melody.)

Finding Bandmates

Where can you find additional personnel who have the instrumental and/or vocal skills you need to complete your band?

MOST MUSIC STORES HAVE POSTER BOARDS AVAILABLE FOR AREA MUSICIANS TO ADVERTISE THEIR SERVICES, FIND OR OFFER INSTRUMENT INSTRUCTION, AND ANNOUNCE UPCOMING PERFORMANCES.

Most band members are friends—or friends of friends. Let your schoolmates know you want to start a band. Also, discuss it with the school music faculty. They may know of talented students who might be interested in joining you.

Music stores are logical places to meet other musicians. Tell the staff your plans. Spend time hanging out there, listening to customers who come in to try out instruments or, like you, just hang out.

Post fliers on bulletin boards at school, music stores, coffee shops, music clubs, and other places where musicians frequent. Place classified ads in school or community newspapers.

What's Your Genre?

What style of music do you want to play? To a great degree, that will determine the combination of instruments you'll need in your band.

Rock and Country

The most common rock band configuration is the same today as it was in the 1950s and 1960s: electric guitar, drums, bass guitar, and rhythm guitar. Some bands have no interest in vocal music and focus exclusively on a loud, driving, metallic sound. Others craft instrumental arrangements mainly to back vocalists.

Many rock bands use additional instruments. Even those who stick to the basic four in live performances usually supplement their arrangements with other instruments when they record.

Contemporary country bands have much the same instrumental makeup as rock bands. They feature strong vocalists. Most country groups use acoustic rhythm guitars. Special instruments that define the country sound are pedal steel guitar, fiddle, and harmonica.

Pop

Pop bands typically cover hit songs. Vocalists are vital in most pop groups. Piano or electronic keyboard is the essential instrument in many pop bands because it gives them variety. They generally draw material from multiple styles—rock, light jazz, country, soul, and reggae. A skilled keyboardist can imitate most of the instruments used on the original recordings, including drums and percussion. Some performing acts consist of just one or two vocalists backed by a keyboardist.

Blues and Jazz

Blues and jazz acts generally include drums, electric or acoustic bass, rhythm guitar, and a featured lead instrument. The lead may be electric guitar, horn or woodwind, or piano/keyboard. The group may use other instruments and feature one or more vocalists.

This style of music is known for soloists' improvisations. They play by "feeling" the music, and each performance

FROM GARAGE TO GREATNESS

Some of the most popular rock bands of the past fifty years started as garage bands. The most famous was the Beatles.

John Lennon, Paul McCartney, and George Harrison began performing in Liverpool, England, in a skiffle band called the Quarrymen. (The original Quarrymen, organized by Lennon, actually had to practice in a small backyard bomb shelter because of the noise they made.) They were in their mid-teens.

The musicians jammed for long hours at a time. Over the next five years, they performed regularly in Liverpool and Hamburg, Germany, developing their distinct sound and changing personnel. Drummer Ringo Starr joined in 1962, the year they began recording as the Beatles. Within a year, they were internationally famous.

Other noted bands that began with informal rehearsals include the Rolling Stones.

Tokio Hotel is an example of a twenty-first-century garage band that has made it big. The band originated in Germany in 2001, when its members were between ten and thirteen years old. They began their rise to success by performing gigs around their small hometown of Magdeburg.

THE BEATLES, ON THE BRINK OF WORLD FAME, PERFORM AT A LIVERPOOL NIGHTCLUB IN EARLY 1962. MANY FANS THINK THEY ENJOYED OVERNIGHT SUCCESS, BUT STARDOM WAS YEARS IN THE MAKING.

is somewhat different. Many specialize in a subcategory of blues, such as classic, urban, boogie-woogie, and jump.

Acoustic Music

Acoustic bands use nonelectric instruments (with the common exception of bass guitar). Some acoustic groups incorporate keyboards. Rather than drums, they usually employ handheld percussive instruments; many use no percussion at all. They focus on vocals and/or solo wizardry on guitar, banjo, mandolin, or fiddle.

Acoustic music flavors include traditional folk (ballads and melodies that may be more than a century old), contemporary folk (modern songs), and bluegrass (noted for fiddle, banjo, and mandolin instrumentation and high, nasal vocals). Some duos, trios, and other small ensembles perform acoustic pop—chart hits rendered with acoustic instruments.

A few very gifted singers perform in groups with no instruments. Their music is a cappella. They thrive on the unique challenge of entertaining audiences using only their voices. Barbershop quartets are a familiar type of a cappella act. Other groups sing soul, gospel, and novelty songs. One award-winning act, Anonymous 4, explores medieval music from different countries as well as early American hymns.

Other Types of Music

Beach music, gospel, punk, rap, and western swing are only a few of the dozens of musical genres performed today.

25

RISING ABOVE DIFFICULTIES

It's much easier for some young people than others to pursue musical ambitions. Many children in well-to-do households take private music lessons from an early age and receive encouragement from their parents. Others cannot afford to buy a used instrument, much less pay for instruction, and their home life isn't so supportive. Still, they can succeed. (Elvis Presley was born in a two-room house; when he was three, his father was imprisoned for forgery.)

If lack of money is an issue, you may be able to find part-time or temporary work and save enough to buy your instrument. Visit community thrift stores, flea markets, and yard sales. Instruments of excellent quality often are sold for only a few dollars. If one that interests you is slightly damaged, a knowledgeable friend may be able to fix it.

Spread the word about your interest in music. People often give away good instruments they've inherited or no longer use, if they know of a young person who will value the item.

If you are in high school and haven't learned to play a musical instrument yet, don't be discouraged. You haven't missed the boat. Many successful musicians didn't begin to pursue their passions until they were adults.

Increasingly, bands explore alternative or eclectic music—sounds that defy clear definitions.

The Perfect Name

Coming up with a name is a fun aspect of starting a band. Bands find ideas for clever names from countless sources.

Some bands aren't picky about a name, as long as it's original. They might look no farther than their neighborhood and call themselves the Hillbrook Sound Machine, Mason Street Girls Club, or Noise from the Northside. Brian Compton, a Berkeley, California, bassist who has started several bands since high school, fondly remembers his college group: Doublewide, so-named for the doublewide home the student musicians rented.

Your name may suggest the style of music you play. Sour Mash, for example, was the name of a bluegrass-rock band. The name doesn't have to reflect your sound, but it shouldn't suggest the *wrong* sound. (A rap group will be ill served by a name like the Electronic Swing Romance. A new group that debuts as the Great Metal Reef will draw blank stares from the audience if it plays acoustic pop.)

Family bands may use a family name or connection. Three Florida siblings called their pop-calypso trio Chuffa—the name of their dog.

Some names say nothing about the band's style of music but pique curiosity. A few examples include Rascal Flatts, Reckless Kelly, and Pirates of the Mississippi.

Finally, there are bands whose names are so innocuous that they command subtle respect—assuming the musicians demonstrate excellence. Consider the Zac Brown Band, a top country recording and performing act. A California dance band calls itself simply the Garage Band. In 1961, a band formed as the Hawks for the purpose of backing up a Canadian rock singer, Ronnie Hawkins. From the mid-1960s to the mid-1970s, it backed up Bob Dylan using a new name: The Band.

Be Original

When thinking about the kind of music you want to create, remember the importance of originality. Some local and regional bands perform only covers of recorded hits. Beach bands, for example, play at clubs and parties where people expect to dance to beach standards.

Although some musicians earn a good living playing covers, no band has become famous by imitating another band. When recording stars cover songs that were made famous by other artists, they do the songs their own way. The ability to function as a "human jukebox"—playing hit requests—will get you some local gigs, but never a recording contract.

Don't expect to establish your hallmark sound at your first rehearsal. It will develop over time. Dare to experiment, and keep an open ear to each band member's ideas.

GETTING DOWN TO WORK

Now that you have begun to master an instrument and have found other musicians with a common interest, the work begins. Hours, days, weeks, months—perhaps years—of band rehearsals are in the offing before you'll be ready to entertain.

Stephen Anderson, author of *So, You Wanna Be a Rock Star?*, explains the difference between "practice" and "rehearsal." "Practice is what you do on your own to become better at your individual instrument," he says. "Rehearsal is when your whole band gets together to work on your sound and your performance as a group."

CHAPTER THREE

GARAGE BAND PASS

MORE THAN MUSIC IS INVOLVED IN BAND WORK. HERE, A TEEN BAND IN FLORIDA SETS UP AND TUNES IN PREPARATION FOR A PERFORMANCE AT A WEEKLY LIBRARY EVENT.

Where to Rehearse?

Not all garage bands are literally that. Some rehearse in basements, living rooms, dens, and bedrooms. Actually, a basement may be best for a rock band. Since it's at least partly underground, it reduces the neighborhood noise problem.

Places outside the home may also be available. For example, a community organization such as the YMCA or a local recreation center may provide a vacant area in return for your occasional performances at fund-raising events. A friend or relative who owns an industrial facility or warehouse (out of hearing of residential neighborhoods) might allow you to set up in an unused room or corner.

If you live in a large city, commercial practice space is probably available. Brian Compton, the California bassist, is now in a band called Stealing West, which frequently opens for well-known touring acts. Stealing West rehearses in "a crazy warehouse in Oakland that has been partitioned into about fifty practice rooms."

Wherever you practice, consider the effects of your sound on people within hearing. Loud music that excites you might be infuriating to them.

Electric bass is the most conspicuous rehearsal instrument. Its throbbing, pounding sound can be as booming to people a block away as it is to the musicians in the basement. Turn the volume down until performance time.

Drums and electric guitars can also be disruptive. Guitars, like basses, can be turned down. Little can be done to reduce the volume of percussion instruments, but you can take measures to soundproof the rehearsal hall. Sound-reduction material that's available commercially can be expensive. Cheap or free alternatives for absorbing sound include carpets, egg cartons, and wall blankets.

HOW LONG MUST YOU PRACTICE AND REHEARSE?

Your band doesn't have to establish a regular rehearsal schedule. However, a regular schedule will develop the band's sound quicker than a haphazard "whenever we feel like it" approach. It will also reveal early on if any of the musicians lack the commitment to succeed.

How often and long should you practice, individually and as a group? It depends on how good you want to be. A typical band may hold a four-hour rehearsal every Saturday and expect each member to practice privately at least an hour a day. Some bands rehearse two or three times a week.

Consider that many college majors in music performance (violin, piano, etc.) practice from eighteen to twenty hours each week. Malcolm Gladwell, author of *The Outliers*, concluded from his research that ten thousand hours of preparation/practice is the benchmark for success. That is, people in any profession or endeavor—including music—will work at it about that long before they can consider themselves really good at what they're doing. Simple math shows that if you apply yourself to practice twenty hours a week, fifty weeks out of the year, it will take you ten years to excel at your music.

Most garage band members quickly realize they have other interests in life. They decide they don't need to be the very best musicians on the planet. Still, they can continue to develop, perform, and enjoy their music.

There is such a thing as too much practice. Marty Jourard, author of *Start Your Own Band*, points out the risk of working on a song until you're sick of it—before you even perform it. "You want to play with a certain energy and edge to your performance, and rehearsing six days a week will definitely dull this edge."

Make the Most of Your Rehearsal Time

It's easy to squander valuable rehearsal time. Bandmates like to chat and catch up on the latest personal news, and there's nothing wrong with a little clowning around.

A problem with some garage bands is that they do little besides socialize and jam aimlessly. They show up for a rehearsal with no goal. They spend two, three, or four hours just "going with the flow."

The bands that make the fastest progress are those that plan their rehearsals. Rehearsal plans follow different patterns, depending on the group's stage of progress.

In the beginning days and weeks, a good objective is to work on just three or four songs until they're in roughly presentable form. Then introduce a new song. Spend some of your time focusing on it; spend other time reviewing and polishing earlier material. As each piece falls into place, add new pieces.

In your rehearsal structure, pencil in time for jamming. Jamming is important for creativity and defining the band's sound. But assign it a time—perhaps half an hour, perhaps an hour—during the rehearsal.

Some bands find it practical to spend the first part of the rehearsal reviewing familiar songs, then jamming, and finally examining something new. Others prefer to loosen up in a freewheeling jam before applying themselves to specific songs. Still others like to do all the serious work first and then wind down the session in an open jam.

A ROCK BAND REHEARSES IN A STUDIO. TO MAKE THE MOST OF YOUR TIME TOGETHER, IT'S IMPORTANT TO PLAN REHEARSALS MUCH LIKE YOU PLAN PERFORMANCES.

At the end of each rehearsal, decide what you will work on next time. Write it down, and stick to your written work plan.

Usually, one band member assumes the role of rehearsal manager and, by extension, becomes the band's leader. This person is not necessarily the lead musician. In fact, the lead musician is probably too concentrated on his or her sound to function well as the group leader.

Choose Your Repertoire Carefully

Whether you're going to perform original music or covers of hit songs, consider each number thoughtfully. Discuss it as a

34

group. Band members may toy with dozens of songs before choosing the dozen that are best for them.

In a successful performance, each song contributes to the band's overall sound. Each delivers something of interest to the audience. If a song in your repertoire fails to do that, discard it.

Recording your rehearsals can help reveal weak songs—personal favorites that actually have little entertainment value and will be worthless to your act. After hours and weeks rehearsing it, a song might become more important to certain musicians than it should be. Band members sometimes become so fiercely proud of their individual contributions to a song that they fail to realize that the song overall is a boring dud.

Take Advantage of Technology

Computerization and advances in electronics have introduced new—and often inexpensive—conveniences to all aspects of life. Technology is especially useful to musicians.

Recording devices, for example, are both cheap and sophisticated. It's a good idea to make audio—or, better, audiovisual—recordings of songs you're rehearsing. This exposes weaknesses and problems that you may not detect while you're playing the song. Listening closely to a replay can show you exactly where you need to improve.

Musical technology also includes powerful tools such as computerized keyboards. Musicians can record instrument tracks one at a time and create "packaged" arrangements.

MUSIC-RELATED COMPUTER PROGRAMS ARE POWERFUL AND FUN TO USE.
WITH ONE TYPE OF SOFTWARE, FOR EXAMPLE, MUSICIANS CAN MIX
THEIR RECORDING TRACKS AT A COMPUTER KEYBOARD.

Powerful editing software is available for mixing recorded soundtracks. Some programs, such as Audacity, can be downloaded for free.

Buying Equipment

Each musician, of course, personally owns an instrument. Meanwhile, the band will begin to acquire mutual equipment. You should decide in the beginning such questions as how to pay for it, where to keep it, and how to transport it.

A sound system is the big item. It includes an electronic soundboard, main and monitor speakers, microphones and earphones, stands, and cords. Smaller, less expensive items include metronomes and electronic tuners.

It's certainly convenient if one band member already owns some or all of the needed equipment. The group should discuss, though, how that person will be compensated if the band begins performing for pay. And what will happen to the band if that individual leaves?

Many bands establish a fund for purchasing equipment. As the band begins to perform, a share of the earnings should go into the fund to buy better and additional equipment. It's also wise to keep a petty cash fund for gas and other travel expenses.

A very important tip is to choose good equipment. Your personal instruments should be easy to play and deliver excellent sound. Likewise, good band equipment is essential. Cheaply manufactured microphones and amplifiers will hurt your sound and won't last long.

GETTING ALONG

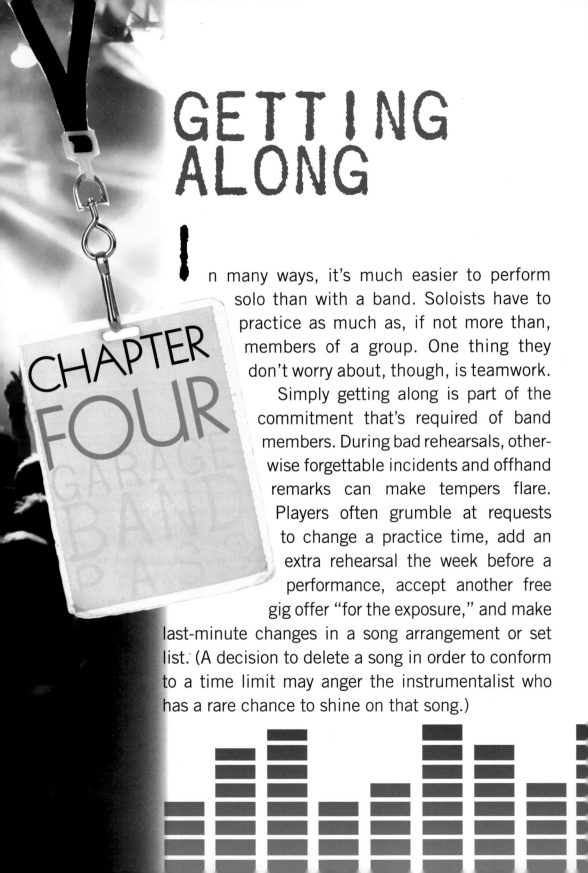

CHAPTER FOUR

In many ways, it's much easier to perform solo than with a band. Soloists have to practice as much as, if not more than, members of a group. One thing they don't worry about, though, is teamwork. Simply getting along is part of the commitment that's required of band members. During bad rehearsals, otherwise forgettable incidents and offhand remarks can make tempers flare. Players often grumble at requests to change a practice time, add an extra rehearsal the week before a performance, accept another free gig offer "for the exposure," and make last-minute changes in a song arrangement or set list. (A decision to delete a song in order to conform to a time limit may anger the instrumentalist who has a rare chance to shine on that song.)

Typical complaints heard among band members:

- "The drummer plays too loud."
- "The bassist fumbles the beat."
- "The harmony vocalist sings flat."
- "The lead guitarist is never in tune. He should learn to hear better or buy a decent instrument."
- "She keeps insisting we learn a song the rest of us don't like."

Egos, Conflicts, Bad Habits, and Other Challenges

It's been said that living with a roommate in a dorm or apartment is much like being married. The same can be said of joining a band. Even among musicians who share identical musical interests, personalities can annoy.

Egos become problems if one player is an excellent musician (or thinks so) and the others are mediocre. They also get in the way if an individual believes he or she is the best judge of appropriate material to include in the act, or the ideal arrangements. Overly headstrong musicians make better soloists than bandmates.

Diverse musical interests can add originality and depth to the band's sound. Often, though, musical differences in taste result in incompatibility. When conflicts arise, compromises are necessary. If a member stubbornly resists compromise, the band may be forced to redefine its makeup.

IT'S ESSENTIAL FOR BAND MEMBERS TO REMAIN ON FRIENDLY TERMS. BAD HABITS, FROM SELFISH ATTITUDES TO SUBSTANCE ABUSE, HAVE BROKEN UP MANY MUSICALLY GIFTED GROUPS.

Bad personal habits cause problems in many bands. Behavioral issues include laziness, chronic tardiness, short tempers, and substance abuse (including smoking). In some bands, one individual—an exceptional instrumentalist or singer, owner of the sound system, resident of the practice venue—is vital. For that reason, other members tend to make special allowances. In time, though, preferential treatment almost invariably causes the relationship to collapse.

Another major cause of discontent is discouragement. The real test of togetherness comes when the band seems to be

DRAW UP A BAND CONSTITUTION

At the beginning, few garage players think of the band as a business. They just want to get together and have fun with their music.

If you sense a potential for work to be found and money to be made, you should think about the business angles and potential problems. Donald S. Passman is an entertainment lawyer and author of *All You Need to Know About the Music Business*. He says, "The time to make an agreement among yourselves is now, when everybody is all friendly and kissy-face."

Put in writing what will happen, for example, if a band member departs. A member might leave not because of unhappiness but for ordinary reasons (relocation, going off to college, developing other interests). If the band has jointly invested in equipment, the members should decide in advance how to compensate a member who leaves.

It's also a good idea to draw up a personal contract with your parents. In it, for example, promise to keep up your school studies and other important activities. Vow to keep your room clean and continue performing your assigned chores. Assure them that you won't keep them awake by practicing late on your electric guitar, booming bass, or drums. Promise you won't fall in with the "wrong crowd." A written contract with your parents can help win their support for your dream.

making no progress, is being offered no serious gigs, or has a bad performing experience such as a small or unreceptive audience.

Divide the Work

Organization will serve any new band well—unless you have no desire ever to get out of the garage. Most garage bands have greater ambitions. In order to attain them, everyone must pitch in to do the behind-the-scenes (nonperformance) work. With thoughtful organization, these tasks can be not only tolerable but also fun. Routine chores include:

- Transporting equipment, setting it up, and taking it down.
- Tuning stringed instruments. Instrumentalists are expected to know how to tune, but for some—including highly skilled performers—tuning is a challenge.
- Cleaning up the rehearsal mess. If a parent happens into the rehearsal garage or basement between sessions and encounters a litter of paper cups, cigarette butts, spitballs, and damaged furniture, you may lose your rehearsal venue.
- Creating attractive flyers, writing press announcements and fact sheets, and finding media and advertising outlets to announce the band's availability.
- Keeping records. This will become essential when the band begins performing for pay and investing in equipment.

You should make use of each bandmate's talents, musical or otherwise. If a member of the band loves to exhibit his physical prowess, put him in charge of equipment. If one has perfect pitch, make her the official instrument tuner.

A BASSIST USES AN ELECTRONIC TUNER TO FIND THE PRECISE PITCH FOR EACH STRING. EVEN WITH SUCH AIDS, FINE-TUNING IS A CONSTANT TASK FOR PLAYERS OF STRINGED INSTRUMENTS.

If one has artistic and/or writing talents, there's your public relations chief. A mate with good math skills is the likely candidate for organizing schedules and tracking expenses and earnings.

Players who have outgoing personalities may be the ones who begin getting gigs—the band's de facto "agents" (although every member should be on the lookout for performance possibilities). A member with exceptional charisma should be groomed to become the onstage front—the one who introduces songs, cracks jokes, and otherwise fills up those dreaded voids of silence during a show.

Remember to Have Fun Together

Band membership requires work and sacrifice, but it should also be fun. The band should make time away from the garage or other rehearsal setting to enjoy life together. Go to a movie, go bowling, go out for a pizza blast, or go hiking or biking or camping.

You can combine pleasure with your musical pursuits. Attend concerts and local shows as a group. Spend time just sitting around listening to one another's music collections.

It's easy to become discouraged in a band. Musicians grow disgusted and weary in the face of repeated hassles, especially if they seem to be making little progress. They tire of playing songs suggested by other band members— songs they don't particularly enjoy. They complain that certain partners get their way most of the time. They realize one or two of the others are essentially lazy, refusing to improve their skills and thus holding back the band. They wonder why they're investing so much time in a band full of problems.

To keep things in perspective, it's helpful to take a break from the work and enjoy one another's friendship. (It also helps if you can look past one another's flaws and focus on the strengths.)

Know When to Quit

Some bands stay together forty years or longer. Others last forty minutes or fewer. Musicians may find it impossible to put down their passion for as long as they live, or they may decide at an early stage that other things are more important to them. Ultimately, all bands come to an end.

There are many reasons why young bands break up. Key members may go off to college, or their families may relocate. Their musical tastes may change. They may realize that they have less energy to pursue perfection and stardom than their partners. Some groups disband because the players simply fail to get along.

It's important to keep the band experience in balance with the rest of your life. If it becomes all-consuming, maybe it isn't what you should be doing. Individual musicians and the band as a whole should regularly evaluate how far the band has come and where it appears to be going. As the music evolves, the band may veer into a direction that doesn't appeal to an individual member. If so, it may be time for the player to move into a new phase of musical development—perhaps to join a different band.

An ancient proverb advises: "When you come to the last page, close the book."

GOING PUBLIC

CHAPTER FIVE

How do you know when it's time for your band to go public? How many months of rehearsal are required? How many stage-ready songs must you prepare? How much stage equipment do you need?

The answers might relieve you: It depends, it depends, it depends, and it depends.

Some bands have gotten gigs—paying gigs, in some instances—before they've become bands. A band's birth story might go something like this:

A parent, parent of a friend, schoolteacher, neighbor, etc., is aware of your developing skills as a pianist, guitarist, and/or singer. This person is planning some small event (house party, birthday party, end-of-season cookout for the cross-country team, church dinner) and it would be nice to have background entertainment. "Would you be available to set up in a corner of the room [or end of the lawn] and play a few songs? You can just play three or four and repeat them once or twice between seven and nine o'clock. We can pay you $75."

You're shy, but you'll do anything for money. And you do love music. And you do believe you have talent.

You think of a friend who's been learning electric bass and is pretty good already or another friend who can sing radio hits just like the recording artists. You have two weeks to prepare. By involving a partner or two, you'll be under less personal pressure.

So you get together and come up with several slightly rough but presentable song arrangements. You smile as you perform them for a milling audience that doesn't seem to be paying attention…until the end of the evening, when your host thanks you for your talented contribution to the event and you receive an enthusiastic round of applause— and several people approach and ask where they can come to hear you play again.

Voilà! A band is born.

Other bands begin methodically. They get together in a garage with the purpose of forging a good sound together. They don't even think about gigs until they're confident they have something good—and original—for people to hear.

Getting Gigs

When you're ready to perform, it isn't difficult to find places to do so—although there may be little or no money in it at first. Possible venues for beginning bands include talent shows; school dances; community, civic, and church events; open mike nights at music clubs; coffee shops that cater especially to young customers; mall promotions; and fairs and carnivals.

A SINGER-SONGWRITER PERFORMS ORIGINAL MUSIC AT A POPULAR NEW YORK CLUB. LISTENING ROOMS IN MANY CITIES GIVE NEW MUSICIANS THE STAGE ON OPEN MIKE NIGHTS.

Volunteer to entertain for free at school and community events. Sign up for band competitions. Even if you don't win or place, you may catch the notice of people who are looking for entertainers.

Send a letter or flyer to your local chamber of commerce. Most businesses in town are chamber members, and they occasionally sponsor social events for employees, customers, potential new customers, and other businesses.

Don't expect immediate stardom, even locally. Be prepared for embarrassments, poor performances, and other discouragements. As you'll soon discover, amplifier fuses blow, vocalists have coughing spells, stage lights can behave weirdly, sound technicians sometimes turn the wrong dials at the wrong times, special effects can sound ineffective, and promising gigs can get canceled for myriad reasons.

Chin up. You're only beginning. There will be other shows to perform.

Stage Fright?

There are musicians who never have known stage fright. They were born to perform.

Most, though, require some confidence building. Even the most gifted, well-trained musicians usually begin their careers nervously. Some will experience a bit of stage fright before every performance for as long as they live. But most performers will lose the worst of their anxiety after a few successful engagements.

Two things can help you conquer stage fright: 1) the confidence that you can perform a piece of music (almost) flawlessly and 2) experience onstage.

The ultimate advice for a performer before taking the stage—whether it's a sidewalk fund-raiser or an auditorium concert—is the old scouting motto: be prepared. You should know your part well enough to perform it forward and backward wearing a blindfold and earplugs. That requires diligent practice.

A safe course is to start with small audiences—a handful of friends or relatives gathered in your garage to hear the band run through its show nonstop, mistakes and all. Then look for casual opportunities to perform: a family or neighborhood cookout, a pool party, a sidewalk sale. Simply get used to having friends, then strangers, pay attention to you and the music you perform. Soon, you'll realize that you can do this, no matter where you're performing or how large the audience.

From the beginning, work on your stage presence. For example, don't bashfully hang your head while performing. Look out at the audience. If you're too shy to make eye contact, focus your gaze slightly above the heads of the people.

How Much Are You Worth?

At an early point, you'll have to determine what your sound is worth monetarily. How much should you charge?

A SINGER–GUITARIST PERFORMS WITH A BAND AT A CONCERT IN INDIANA. ONE APPEAL OF A GOOD BAND IS THE VISIBLE SINCERITY OF ITS MUSICIANS.

Bands usually establish a flat fee. To arrive at it, decide how much each member wants to be paid, how much you want to put into your bank account (equipment fund), and what expenses you typically will incur.

Example: A new four-member band wants to earn $50 per player per gig. That's $200. Add at least another full share for the piggybank (your group fund) and $50 for transportation expenses (you'll probably need to ride in two or more vehicles). Your standard fee therefore is $300.

Make it negotiable. If you'll be playing for a private audience of several dozen, or if you're needed only for one twenty-minute set at a convention or program, you might consider lowering your fee. Don't underprice your band, though. Even for a cameo performance, you should be compensated for your travel expenses. You should also be paid for the time it will take you to set up and take down your equipment.

What's Your Musical Future?

Make an honest assessment of your new band's talent and potential. If you genuinely see promise, begin thinking about your group's future.

On the other hand, you may wish to remain a garage band just for fun, performing occasionally for the enjoyment and extra income.

Your musical ambitions may lie somewhere in between. Some musicians have no illusions of becoming rock stars or even self-supporting performers, but they love to investigate

MAKING YOUR BAND FAMOUS

Start by making your group famous locally. Spread the word about your band's availability by posting to public bulletin boards, networking online, and distributing flyers. When you get a gig, even a small one, announce it via the local newspaper and broadcast media. Do everything you can think of to broaden awareness of your music and your band's name.

Beginning bands today have a "reach" that was undreamed of a few years ago. The Internet is a promotional medium like none before—and free to use, for the most part.

Keep all of your Facebook and Twitter friends informed of your musical activities. Post demo recordings and performance video clips on YouTube (being careful not to violate copyright laws). Establish fan sites on MySpace and Facebook. Introduce each member of your group to the Internet public. Post fresh information about your band weekly, if not daily.

As you build a fan base, always bear in mind the value of your supporters. A band-fan relationship should be mutual. Show your supporters that you appreciate and respect them. Your first fans can bring you new fans.

Spend a little time with younger followers especially. If they indicate an interest in guitar playing, show them a chord or two between sets or after the show. Encouraging other aspiring musicians can win you a lot more fans and friends than you suspect.

new sounds. Electric bassist Brian Compton, now in his early thirties, has started four bands in four cities where he's lived. The first was in high school, the second in college, the third while he was in his mid-twenties. Today, his work is well known in the San Francisco Bay area.

THIS PERFORMER HAS CDS, STICKERS, AND BUSINESS CARDS AVAILABLE WHEREVER SHE PERFORMS. CONSTANT PERSONAL PROMOTION IS THE KEY TO SUCCESS FOR YOUNG MUSICIANS WHILE THEY ARE ESTABLISHING THEMSELVES.

Music is not his livelihood; Compton has a day job as a digital media specialist for a public relations firm. But music is a big part of his life. Each of his bands, he says, had "a different approach and purpose. All were, in my mind, a success—that is, they served those purposes."

If you consider going pro or semipro, set goals and outline ways in which you can attain them. For example, begin developing contacts within the music business locally, regionally, and nationally. Create a team of dedicated assistants (manager, publicist, etc.) who can help your band reach its goals. Take full advantage of the promotional opportunities offered by the Internet. Research the costs and requirements of recording and publishing original music.

Some bands become full-time professionals in only a year or two, obtaining record contracts, broad airplay, and lucrative tours. For most, the road is much longer and marked by potholes and speed bumps. By the time they succeed, most bands have undergone personnel changes and, in many cases, dramatic changes in their sounds and styles.

Long-term success requires a long-term commitment. At the beginning, the most important thing for a garage band to remember is to have fun with the music.

 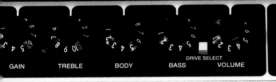

GAIN   TREBLE   BODY   BASS   DRIVE SELECT   VOLUME   REVERB   FOOT SWITCH   VACUUM TUBE DISTORTION   POWER   ON   MADE IN U.S.A.

A CAPPELLA Sung without instrumental accompaniment; literally, "in chapel style."

ACOUSTIC Nonelectric; also, material such as acoustic tile and egg cartons that helps soundproof a room.

AIRPLAY The playing of a song on the radio or other broadcast medium.

AMP (AMPLIFIER) Electrical equipment that makes sound louder.

ARRANGEMENT A band's adaptation of a song, determining the key, instrument and voice combinations, instrumental solo parts, tempo, volume changes, and other elements.

COMBO A small band (combination of musicians).

COMPENSATE To pay or repay someone for work or property.

COVER The rerecording or performance of a song previously recorded or performed by someone else; to rerecord or perform previously introduced music.

DE FACTO In practice.

DEMO A demonstration recording produced not for sale, but in hopes of obtaining a recording contract or gig.

GENRE A category of music, art, or literature.

GIG A live performance or series of regular performances.

GROUPIE A devout fan who attends a band's performances whenever possible.

IMPROVISATION The performance of music offhand, without prearrangement.

INCUR To become burdened with something, such as a debt.

INNOCUOUS Unexceptional; inoffensive.

LUCRATIVE Producing a profit or wealth.

METRONOME An electronic device that keeps a musical beat in perfect time.

PEDAL STEEL GUITAR A plucked musical instrument on which the strings' pitches are changed with foot pedals and a sliding finger bar.

PERFECT PITCH The ability to sound and identify a specific musical note without matching it to a tuning device.

REPERTOIRE All the songs a band can play.

RIFF An outstanding instrumental part in a song, typically played on an electric guitar or keyboard.

SET A selection of songs from a band's repertoire that the band intends to play at a given performance or between intermissions.

SKIFFLE An odd, mainly acoustic form of band music played with an uncommon combination of instruments, such as banjo, washboard, harmonica, and jugs.

TRACK One instrumental or vocal part (such as rhythm guitar track, bass track, or lead vocal track) in a blended recording.

VOCALS The singing part or parts (lead voice, possibly with harmony voices) in a band's song arrangement.

Billboard
770 Broadway
New York, NY 10003
(646) 654-4500
Web site: http://www.billboard.com
The "world's premier music publication" is especially noted for
its weekly charts of hits in different categories of music.

Canadian Independent Music Association
30 St. Patrick Street, 2nd Floor
Toronto, ON M5T 3A3
Canada
(416) 485-3152
Web site: http://www.cirpa.ca
This is a trade organization for the independent sector of
the Canadian music and recording industry.

Recording Industry Association of America (RIAA)
1025 F Street NW, 10th Floor
Washington, DC 20004
(202) 775-0101
Web site: http://www.riaa.com
The RIAA is a trade organization for the music industry. Its
Web site includes a page of links to "Legal Music
Sites" for downloading music.

Rolling Stone
1290 Avenue of the Americas
New York, NY 10104
(212) 484-1616
Web site: http://www.rollingstone.com
Rolling Stone is a magazine featuring discussions and news
    concerning popular music and culture.

SPIN
408 Broadway, 4th Floor
New York, NY 10013
(800) 274-7597
Web site: http://www.spin.com
SPIN magazine focuses on rock and alternative rock music.

Women's Audio Mission
1890 Bryant Street, Suite 312
San Francisco, CA 94110
(415) 558-9200
Web site: http://www.womensaudiomission.org
Women's Audio Mission is a nonprofit organization for women
    involved in music production and recording.

Web Sites

Due to the changing nature of Internet links, Rosen Publishing has
developed an online list of Web sites related to the subject of this
book. The site is updated regularly. Please use this link to access
the list:

http://www.rosenlinks.com/gaba/strt

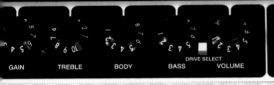

Anderson, Marisa, ed. *Rock 'n Roll Camp for Girls: How to Start a Band, Write Songs, Record an Album and Rock Out!* San Francisco, CA: Chronicle Books, 2008.

Anderson, Stephen. *So, You Wanna Be a Rock Star? How to Create Music, Get Gigs, and Maybe Even Make It BIG!* Hillsboro, OR: Beyond Words Publishing, 1999.

Bliesener, Mark, and Steve Knopper. *The Complete Idiot's Guide to Starting a Band.* New York, NY: Alpha (Penguin Group), 2004.

Buttwinick, Marty. *Starting Your First Band* (The Musicians' How-to Series). Glendale, CA: Sonata Publishing, 2008.

Gipi. *Garage Band.* Translation by Spectrum. New York, NY: First Second Books, 2007.

Hall, Barbara. *Tempo Change.* New York, NY: Delacorte Press, 2009.

Hopper, Jessica. *The Girls' Guide to Rocking: How to Start a Band, Book Gigs, and Get Rolling to Rock Stardom.* New York, NY: Workman Publishing Company, 2009.

Johnson, Arne, and Karen Macklin. *Indie Girl: From Starting a Band to Launching a Fashion Company.* San Francisco, CA: Zest Books (Orange Avenue Publishing), 2008.

Powell, Stephanie. *Hit Me with Music: How to Start, Manage, Record, and Perform with Your Own Rock Band.* Brookfield, CT: Millbrook Press, 1995.

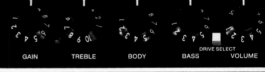

The-Beatles-History.com. "Beatles Timeline." Retrieved
February 2011 (http://www.the-beatles-history.com/
beatles-timeline.html).

The Beatles Web site. Retrieved February 2011 (http://
www.beatles.com).

Bowman, Rob. "Blues." Microsoft Student 2008 [DVD].
Redmond, WA: Microsoft Corporation, 2007.

Citron, Stephen. *Song Writing: A Complete Guide to the
Craft.* New York, NY: Limelight Editions/Hal Leonard
Corporation, 2008.

Gladwell, Malcolm. *The Outliers: The Story of Success.*
New York, NY: Little, Brown and Company, 2008.

Jourard, Marty. *Start Your Own Band: Everything You
Need to Know to Take Your Band to the Top.* New
York, NY: Hyperion, 1997.

Krasilovsky, M. William. *This Business of Music: The
Definitive Guide to the Music Industry.* 9th ed. New
York, NY: Billboard Books/Watson-Guptill
Publications, 2003.

Passman, Donald S. *All You Need to Know About the
Music Business.* New York, NY: Free Press (Simon &
Schuster), 2006.

Unterberger, Richie. "Garage Rock." AllMusic.com.
Retrieved February 2011 (http://www.allmusic.
com/explore/essay/garage-rock-t539).

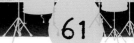

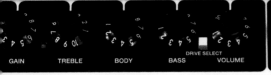

About the Author

Daniel E. Harmon has performed solo and in groups of different genres at festivals, college concerts, nightclubs, school programs, and in other settings. He has composed and recorded sound tracks for public television projects and recorded several albums. A widely published music reviewer and founder of the *Hornpipe* folk music magazine, he has taught several instruments privately and in classes. Harmon is the author of more than seventy books.

Photo Credits

Cover (band), cover and interior background image (club), p. 34 Shutterstock.com; p. 5 Thomas Barwick/Photographer's Choice/Getty Images; p. 9 Digital Vision/Thinkstock; p. 11 Mick Hutson/Redferns/Getty Images; p. 14 Jupiterimages/Photos. com/Thinkstock; pp. 18, 40 Yellow Dog Productions/The Image Bank/Getty Images; p. 20 Douglas Mason/Getty Images; p. 21 Nicole Russo; p. 24 Hulton Archive/Getty Images; p. 30 © St. Petersburg Times/Zuma Press; p. 36 Comstock/Thinkstock; p. 43 © www.istockphoto.com/Don Bayley; pp. 48, 54 Kate Laczynski; p. 51 Joey Foley/FilmMagic/Getty Images; back cover and interior graphic elements: © www.istockphoto.com/Adam Gryko (radio dial), © www.istockphoto.com/Tomasz Zajaczkowski (amp), © www.istockphoto.com/sammyc (drum set silhouette), Shutterstock.com (cable, frequency bar), © www.istockphoto. com/spxChrome (stage pass), © www.istockphoto.com/Bryan Faust (foot pedal).

Designer: Nicole Russo; Editor: Kathy Kuhtz Campbell;
Photo Researcher: Karen Huang